STANDARDS
100 ALL-TIME FAVORITES
VOLUME 3 — S to Y

88 04001

HAL LEONARD PUBLISHING CORPORATION
Home Office: 7777 West Bluemound Road
National Sales Office: 8112 West Bluemound Road
Milwaukee WI 53213
Winona MN 55987

WE KISS IN A SHADOW

(From "THE KING AND I")

Words by OSCAR HAMMERSTEIN II
Music by RICHARD RODGERS

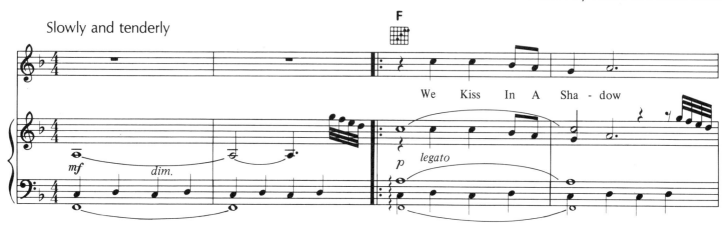

4

sun - light

And say to the sky

Be - hold and be - lieve what you see! Be -

hold how my lov - er loves me!

me!

THAT OLD GANG OF MINE

Words by BILLY ROSE and MORT DIXON
Music by RAY HENDERSON

Slowly

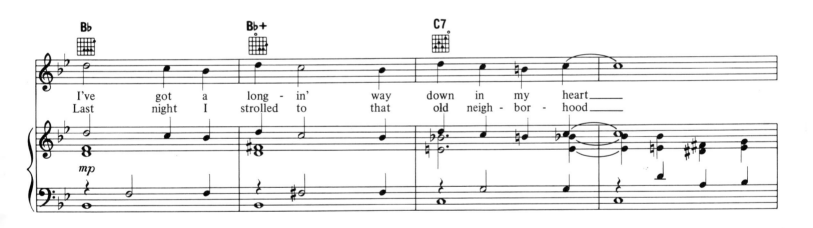

I've got a long-in' way down in my heart
Last night I strolled to that old neigh-bor-hood

For that old gang that has drift-ed a-part
There on that cor-ner I si-lent-ly stood

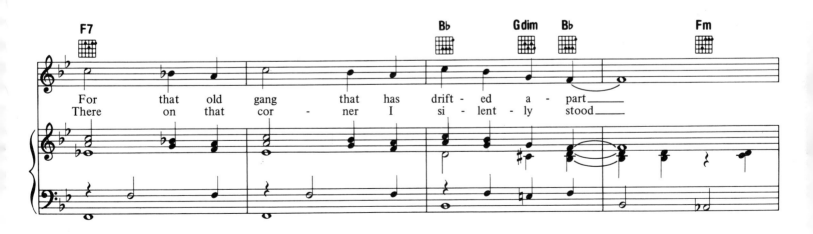

WHEN YOU WISH UPON A STAR
(From Walt Disney's "PINOCCHIO")

Words by NED WASHINGTON
Music by LEIGH HARLINE

TUXEDO JUNCTION

Words by BUDDY FEYNE
Music by ERSKINE HAWKINS, WILLIAM JOHNSON
and JULIAN DASH

SOUTH OF THE BORDER
(Down Mexico Way)

By JIMMY KENNEDY
and MICHAEL CARR

SLEEPY LAGOON

Words by JACK LAWRENCE
Music by ERIC COATES

WITH THESE HANDS

Lyric by BENNY DAVIS
Music by ABNER SILVER

TILL WE TWO ARE ONE

Words by TOM GLAZER
Music by LARRY and BILLY MARTIN

Slowly (with expression)

STAY

Words and Music by MAURICE WILLIAMS

TRY TO REMEMBER

Words by TOM JONES
Music by HARVEY SCHMIDT

WHEN THE RED, RED ROBIN
COMES BOB, BOB, BOBBIN' ALONG

By HARRY WOODS

still I lis - ten for hours and hours.

I'm just a kid a - gain, do - in' what I did a - gain, sing - in' a

song, When The Red, Red Rob - in Comes Bob, Bob, Bob - bin' A -

long.

THERE'LL BE SOME CHANGES MADE

Words by BILLY HIGGINS
Music by W. BENTON OVERSTREET

TILL

Words by CARL SIGMAN
Music by CHARLES DANVERS

YOU DON'T KNOW ME

Words and Music by
CINDY WALKER and EDDY ARNOLD

YELLOW DAYS
La Mentira (Se Te Olvida)

English Words by ALAN BERNSTEIN
Spanish Words & Music by ALVARO CARRILLO

With An Easy Flow

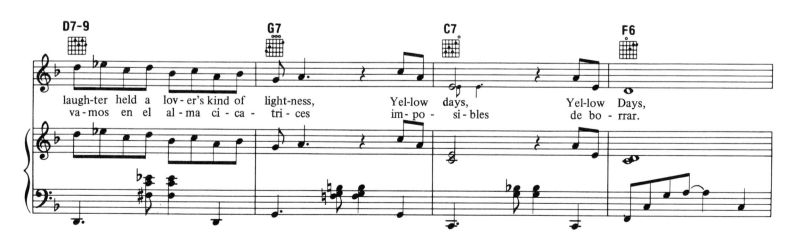

WALK ON THE WILD SIDE

Words and Music by LOU REED

SOFT SHOE SONG
(The Dance My Darlin' Used To Do)

Soft Shoe Tempo

By ROY JORDAN and SID BASS

THE TOUCH OF YOUR LIPS

Words and Music by RAY NOBLE

Moderately Slow with expression

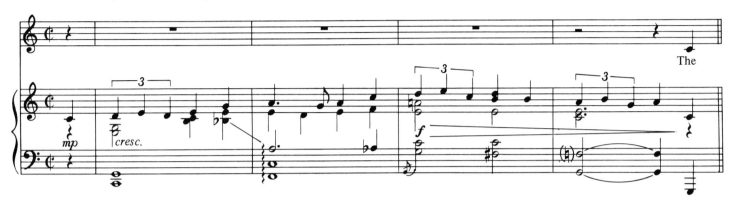

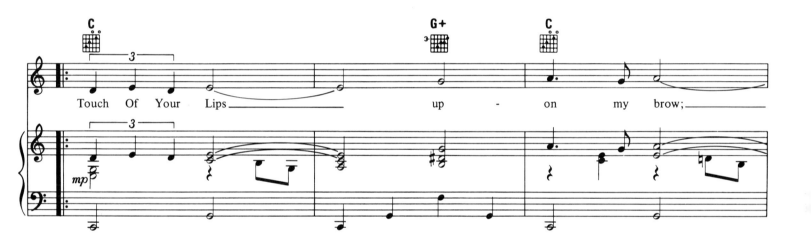

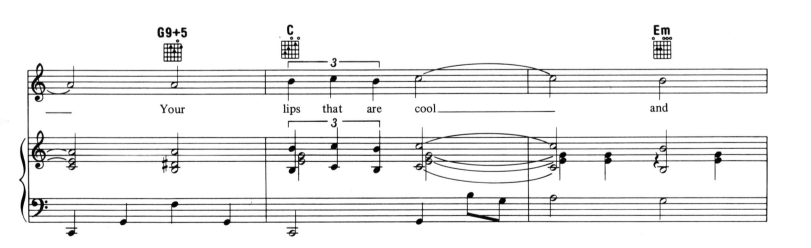

THE THIRD MAN THEME

Words by WALTER LORD
Based on music composed & arranged by ANTON KARAS

56

WILL YOU STILL BE MINE

Words by TOM ADAIR
Music by MATT DENNIS

YOURS

English words by ALBERT GAMSE and JACK SHERR
Spanish Words by AGUSTIN RODRIGUEZ
Music by GONZALO ROIG

SEPTEMBER SONG
(From the Musical Play "Knickerbocker Holiday")

Words by MAXWELL ANDERSON
Music by KURT WEILL

Oh it's a long, long while From May to De-cem-ber,___ But the days grow short,_____ When you reach Sep-tem-ber,___ When the au-tumn wea-ther___ turns the leaves to flame,

'WAY DOWN YONDER IN
NEW ORLEANS

By HENRY CREAMER and J. TURNER LAYTON

SPEAK LOW

Words by OGDEN NASH
Music by KURT WEILL

(I WANNA GO WHERE YOU GO - DO WHAT YOU DO)
THEN I'LL BE HAPPY

Words by SIDNEY CLARE and LEW BROWN
Music by CLIFF FRIEND

Moderately, with a happy beat

WHAT KIND OF FOOL AM I?
(From the Musical Production "STOP THE WORLD - I WANT TO GET OFF")

Words and Music by
LESLIE BRICUSSE
and ANTHONY NEWLEY

73

TWO CIGARETTES IN THE DARK

Words by PAUL FRANCIS WEBSTER
Music by LEW POLLACK

THEM THERE EYES

By MACEO PINKARD, WILLIAM TRACY
and DORIS TAUBER

Moderately, with a Swing beat

78

THIS NEARLY WAS MINE

(From "South Pacific")

Words by OSCAR HAMMERSTEIN II
Music by RICHARD RODGERS

YES SIR, THAT'S MY BABY

By GUS KAHN, WALTER DONALDSON

Moderately, with a bounce

TURN AROUND, LOOK AT ME

By JERRY CAPEHART

Slowly

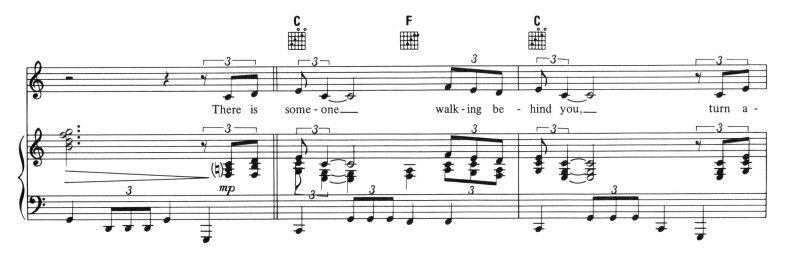

There is some-one ___ walk-ing be - hind you, ___ turn a-

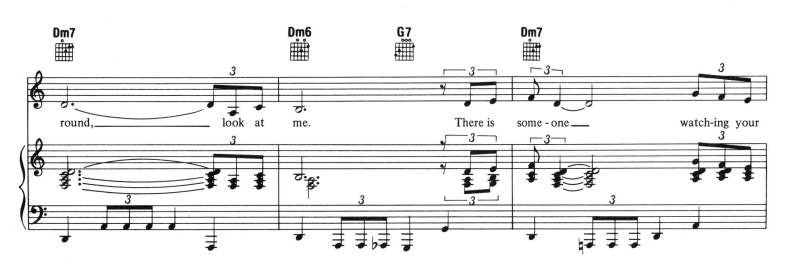

round, ___ look at me. There is some-one ___ watch-ing your

(From "Snow White And The Seven Dwarfs")

SOMEDAY MY PRINCE WILL COME
(Someday I'll Find My Love)

Words by LARRY MOREY
Music by FRANK CHURCHILL

Lyrics:
Some Day My Prince Will Come, Some day one
Some Day I'll find my love, Some

I'll find my love, and how thrilling that the
to call my own, and and I'll know her that the

mo-ment will be, When the prince of my
mo-ment we meet, For my heart will my start

THIS IS MY COUNTRY

Words by DON RAYE
Music by AL JACOBS

YOU ARE WOMAN, I AM MAN

Words by BOB MERRILL
Music by JULE STYNE

Moderately

You Are Wom- an, I Am Man.
You Are Wom- an, I Am Man.

You are small- er, So I can be tall- er than.
You are gen- tle, I am bar- bar- i- an.

93

THERE ARE SUCH THINGS

By STANLEY ADAMS, ABEL BAER
and GEO. W. MEYER

Moderately

You may laugh a-bout Thanks-giv-ing, you may think life is wrong;

but you'll find there's joy in liv-ing when love comes a-long. A heart that's

true,_____ there are such things;_ a dream for

SHOO FLY PIE AND APPLE PAN DOWDY

Words by SAMMY GALLOP
Music by GUY WOOD

Slow bounce

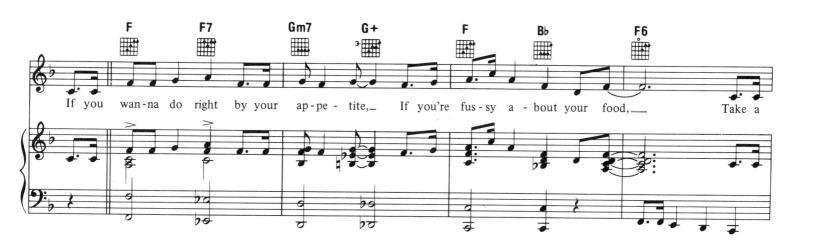

If you wan-na do right by your ap-pe-tite,_ If you're fus-sy a-bout your food,_ Take a

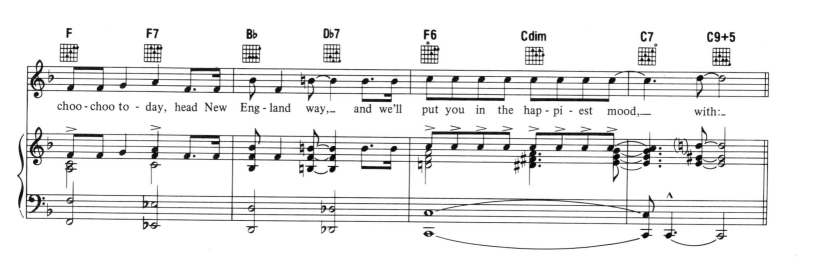

choo-choo to-day, head New Eng-land way,_ and we'll put you in the hap-pi-est mood,_ with:_

YOUNG AT HEART

Words by CAROLYN LEIGH
Music by JOHNNY RICHARDS

WHERE HAVE ALL THE FLOWERS GONE?

Words & Music by PETE SEEGER

Moderately slow, with simplicity

3. Where have all the young men gone? Long time passing.
   Where have all the young men gone? Long time ago.
   Where have all the young men gone?
   They're all in uniform.
   Oh, when will they ever learn?
   Oh, when will they ever learn?

4. Where have all the soldiers gone? Long time passing.
   Where have all the soldiers gone? Long time ago.
   Where have all the soldiers gone?
   They've gone to graveyards, every one.
   Oh, when will they ever learn?
   Oh, when will they ever learn?

5. Where have all the graveyards gone? Long time passing.
   Where have all the graveyards gone? Long time ago.
   Where have all the graveyards gone?
   They're covered with flowers, every one.
   Oh, when will they ever learn?
   Oh, when will they ever learn?

6. Where Have All The Flowers Gone? Long time passing.
   Where Have All The Flowers Gone? Long time ago.
   Where Have All The Flowers Gone?
   Young girls picked them, every one.
   Oh, when will they ever learn?
   Oh, when will they ever learn?

SWEDISH RHAPSODY
(Midsummer Vigil)

English Words by CARL SIGMAN
Music by PERCY FAITH
(Music based on Folk Themes by Hugo Alfven)

One lit - tle fel - low on a Swed - ish street, play - ing sweet, tweet tweet tweet.

One pen - ny whis - tle and an oom - pah beat, Swed - ish Rhap - so - dy.

One lit - tle girl - ie with the gold - en hair, danc - ing there in the square.

tweet tweet tweet. One pen-ny whis-tle and an oom-pah beat,

Swed-ish Rhap-so-dy.

Swed-ish Rhap-so-dy.

TOO FAT POLKA
(She's Too Fat For Me)

By ROSS MacLEAN and ARTHUR RICHARDSON

112

*pronounced "coop"

To last 16 bars of Chorus -

SPANISH HARLEM

Words and Music by
JERRY LEIBER and PHIL SPECTOR

TWILIGHT TIME

Lyric by BUCK RAM
Music by MORTY NEVINS & AL NEVINS

WHEN I'M NOT NEAR THE GIRL I LOVE

Words by E.Y. HARBURG
Music by BURTON LANE

STREETS OF LONDON

Words and Music by RALPH McTELL

3. In the all night café at a quarter past eleven,
   Same old man sitting there on his own.
   Looking at the world over the rim of his teacup,
   Each tea lasts an hour and he wanders home alone.

4. Have you seen the old man outside the seaman's mission,
   Memory fading with the medal ribbons that he wears?
   In our winter city the rain cries a little pity
   For one more forgotten hero and a world that doesn't care.

YOU'RE THE CREAM IN MY COFFEE

Words & Music by B.G. DeSYLVA,
LEW BROWN & RAY HENDERSON

A WORLD OF OUR OWN

Words & Music by TOM SPRINGFIELD

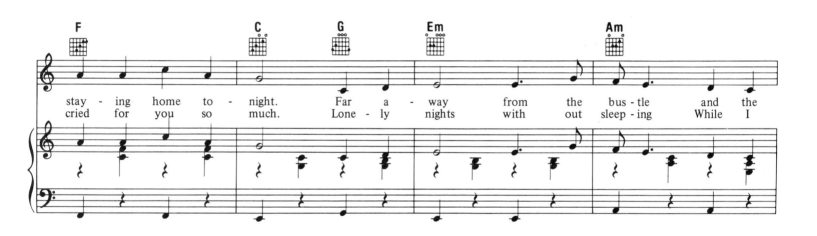

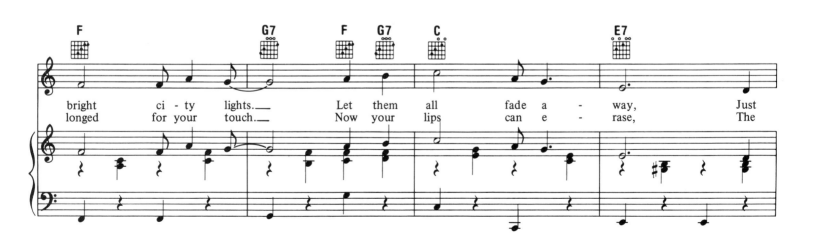

128

WEDDING BELLS
(Are Breaking Up That Old Gang Of Mine)

Words by IRVING KAHAL
and WILLI RASKIN
Music by SAMMY FAIN

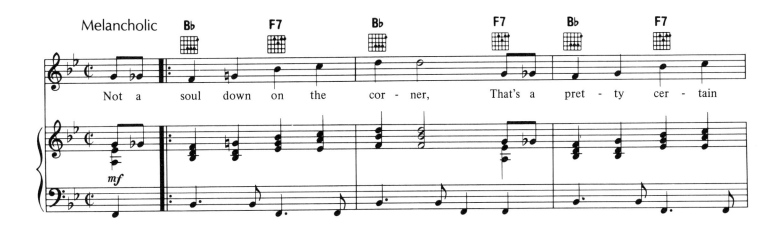

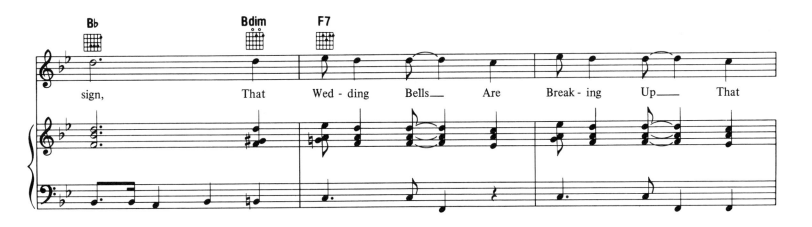

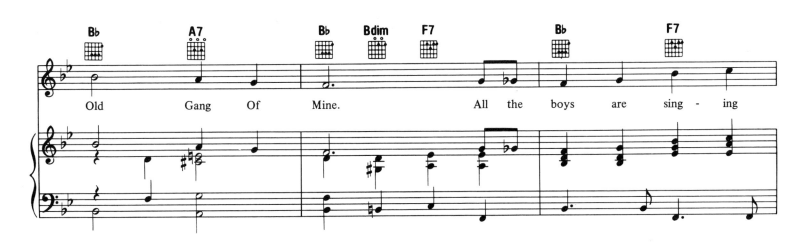

130

THESE FOOLISH THINGS
(REMIND ME OF YOU)

Words by HOLT MARVELL
Music by JACK STRACHEY and HARRY LINK

SWINGING ON A STAR

By JOHNNY BURKE and JIMMY VAN HEUSEN

Two Hearts in Three-Quarter Time

Words and Music by J. YOUNG, R. STOLZ,
W. REISCH and A. ROBINSON

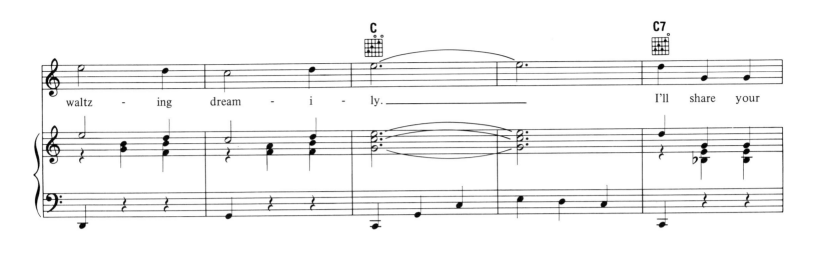

waltz - ing dream - i - ly. _____ I'll share your

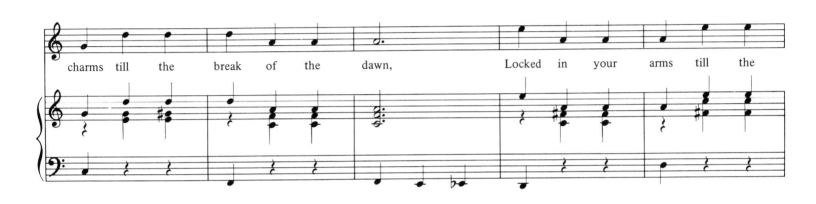

charms till the break of the dawn, Locked in your arms till the

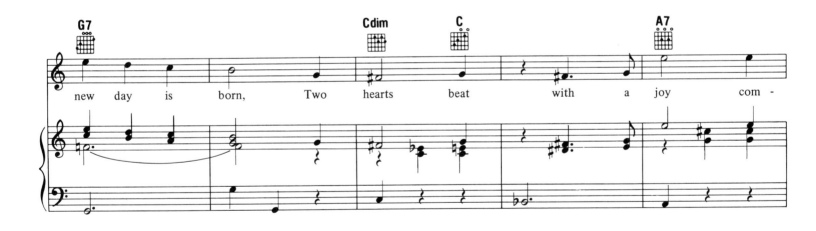

new day is born, Two hearts beat with a joy com -

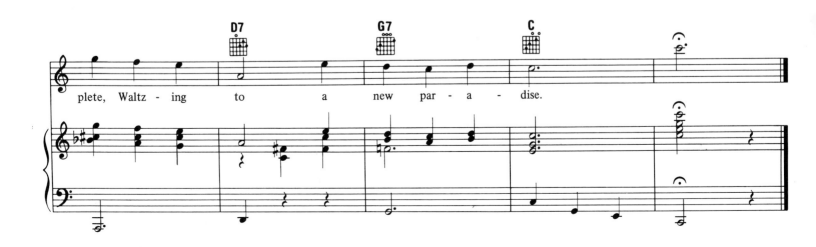

plete, Waltz - ing to a new par - a - dise.

SOMEBODY ELSE IS TAKING MY PLACE

By DICK HOWARD, BOB ELLSWORTH
and RUSS MORGAN

TOO YOUNG

Words by SYLVIA DEE
Music by SID LIPPMAN

WALKIN' MY BABY BACK HOME

Words and Music by ROY TURK
& FRED E. AHLERT

Gee! It's great,__ af-ter be-in' out late,__
Gee! It's great,__ af-ter be-in' out late,__

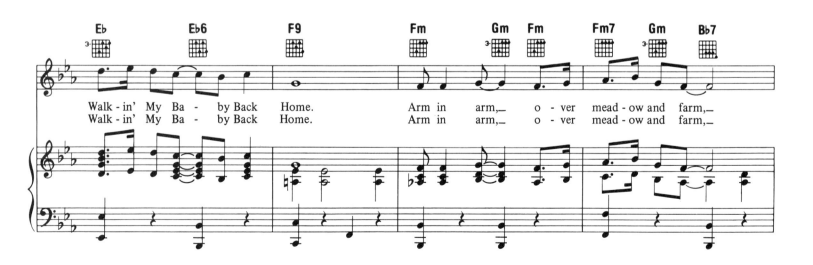

Walk-in' My Ba- by Back Home. Arm in arm,__ o-ver mead-ow and farm,__
Walk-in' My Ba- by Back Home. Arm in arm,__ o-ver mead-ow and farm,__

143

144

SLAUGHTER ON TENTH AVENUE

Music by RICHARD RODGERS

SONGBIRD

Words and Music by
STEVE NELSON and DAVID WOLFERT

150

YOUNG AND FOOLISH

Words by ARNOLD B. HORWITT
Music by ALBERT HAGUE

TO LOVE AGAIN
(Theme From "The Eddy Duchin Story")
Based on Chopin's E flat Nocturne

Words by NED WASHINGTON
Music by MORRIS STOLOFF & GEORGE SIDNEY

155

THE WAY OF LOVE

Original French Lyrics by MICHEL REVGAUCHE
English Lyrics by AL STILLMAN
Music by JACK DIEVAL

STOMPIN' AT THE SAVOY

Words and Music by
BENNY GOODMAN, ANDY RAZAF,
CHICK WEBB and EDGAR SAMPSON

Medium Swing Tempo

THAT'S MY WEAKNESS NOW

By BUD GREEN and SAM H. STEPT

YES, INDEED

By SY OLIVER

With a Slow, measured beat

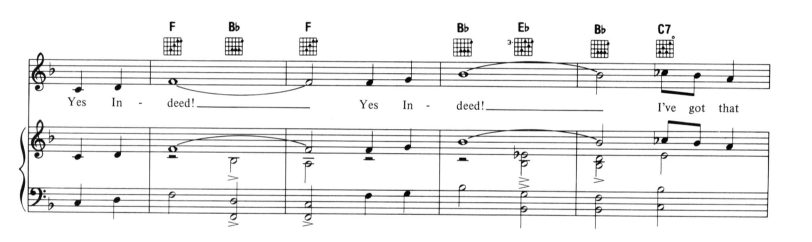

Yes In - deed! _____ Yes In - deed! _____ I've got that

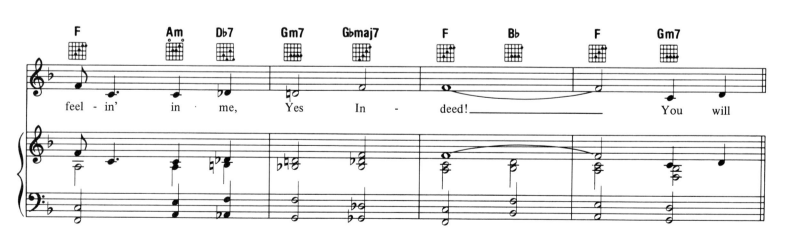

feel - in' in me, Yes In - deed! _____ You will

TRUE LOVE

Moderately Slow

Words and Music by
COLE PORTER

A WALK IN THE BLACK FOREST
(I Walk With You)

Music by HORST JANKOWSKI

STAND BY YOUR MAN

By TAMMY WYNETTE
& BILLY SHERRILL

SILK STOCKINGS

Words and Music by
COLE PORTER

Moderately (With A Latin Feel)

Silk Stock-ings, I touch them and find the joys that re-mind me of you._____ Silk Stock-ings, that give me a-gain Your (Girl){shy}{gay} laugh-ter when they were new._____

THINGS WE DID LAST SUMMER

By SAMMY CAHN, JULE STYNE

You Came A Long Way From St. Louis

Words by BOB RUSSELL
Music by JOHN BENSON BROOKS

WHAT A DIFF'RENCE A DAY MADE

English Words by STANLEY ADAMS
Spanish Words & Music by MARIA GREVER

This Could Be
The Start of Something

Words and Music by STEVE ALLEN

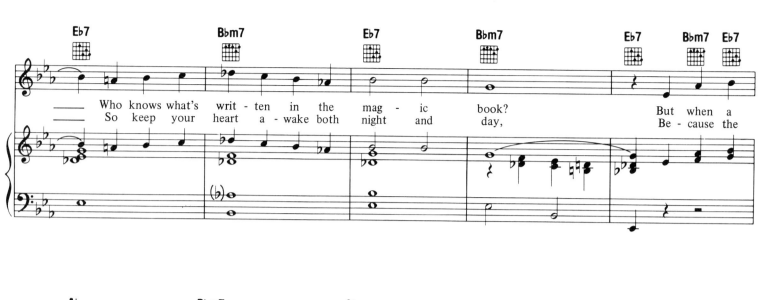

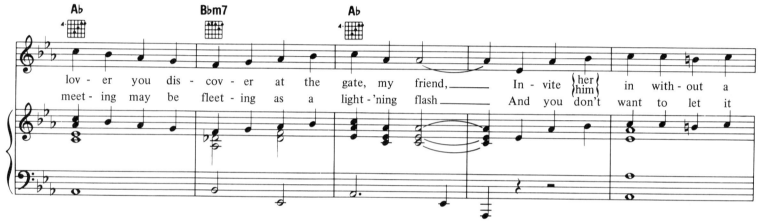

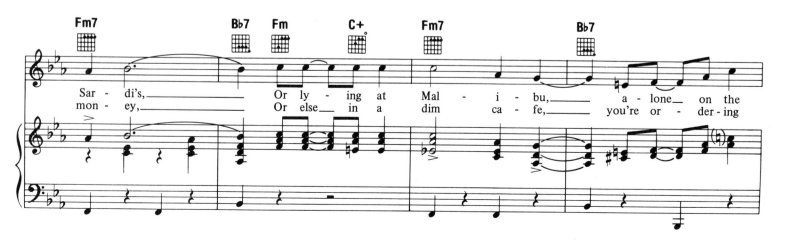

185

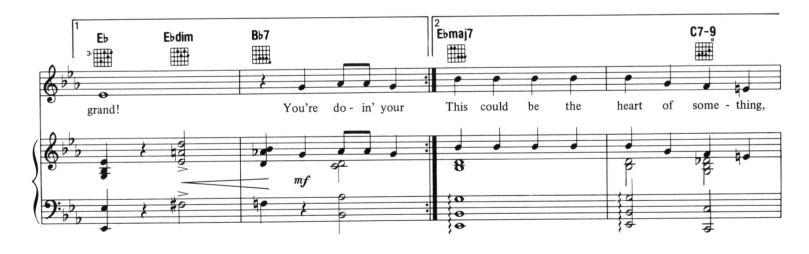

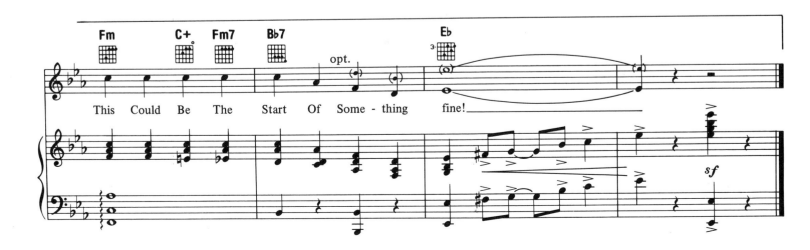

SWEET SOMEONE

Words by GEORGE WAGGNER
Music by BARON KEYES

SMILE
(Theme from "Modern Times")

Words by JOHN TURNER & GEOFFREY PARSONS
Music by CHARLES CHAPLIN

Moderately, with great warmth

Smile, tho' your heart is ach - ing, smile, e - ven tho' it's break - ing.

When there are clouds in the sky, you'll get by, if you smile through your

fear and sor - row, smile and may - be to - mor - row, you'll see the sun come shin - ing

189

YESTERDAY, WHEN I WAS YOUNG
(Hier Encore)

English Lyric by HERBERT KRETZMER
Original French Text and Music by
CHARLES AZNAVOUR

Moderately

SUMMERTIME

Words by DUBOSE HEYWARD
Music by GEORGE GERSHWIN

Moderato (with expression)

193

TUMBLING TUMBLEWEEDS

Words and Music by BOB NOLAN

SONG OF THE ISLANDS

By CHARLES E. KING

Moderately, in a flowing style

Ha-

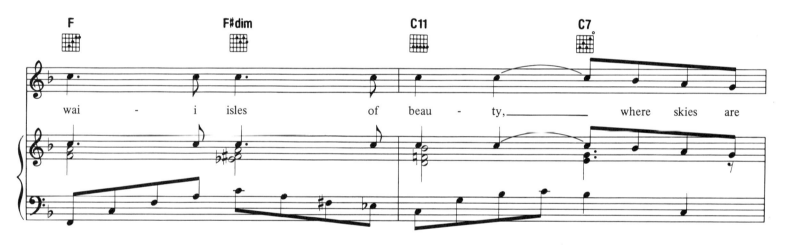

wai - i isles of beau - ty,_____ where skies are

blue and love is true;_____ where balm - y airs and gold - en

THIS IS ALL I ASK
(BEAUTIFUL GIRLS WALK A LITTLE SLOWER)

Words and Music by
GORDON JENKINS

A TASTE OF HONEY

By RIC MARLOW & BOBBY SCOTT

201

WHEN I FALL IN LOVE

Words by EDWARD HEYMAN
Music by VICTOR YOUNG

YOU'RE MY EVERYTHING

Words by MORT DIXON and JOE YOUNG
Music by HARRY WARREN

WITH MY EYES WIDE OPEN, I'M DREAMING

Words by HARRY REVEL
Music by MACK GORDON

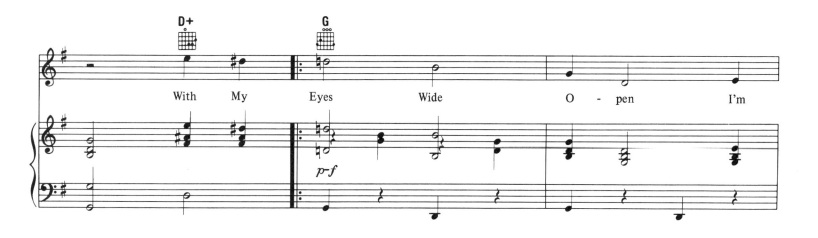

With My Eyes Wide O - pen I'm

Dream - ing, _____ Can it be true I'm hold - ing you Close to my

THIS LOVE OF MINE

Words by FRANK SINATRA
Music by SOL PARKER & HENRY SANICOLA

Expressively

Verse
(ad lib)

Like the moun-tains that reach for the sky, Like the riv - ers that run to the sea;

Slowly, with expression

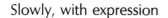

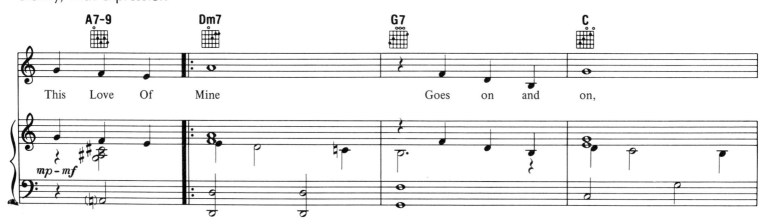

This Love Of Mine Goes on and on,

STAY AS SWEET AS YOU ARE

Words by MACK GORDON
Music by HARRY REVEL

SOMEBODY STOLE MY GAL

Words and Music by LEO WOOD

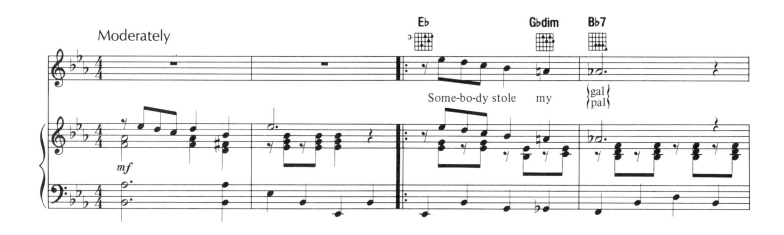

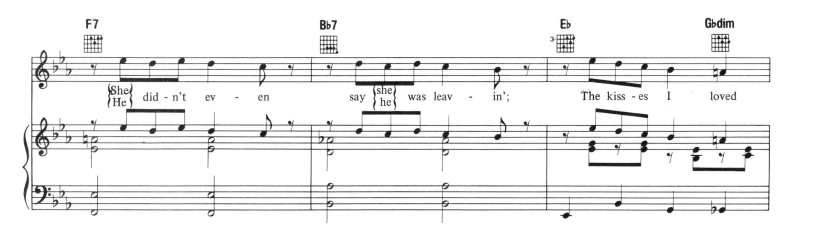

WHERE OR WHEN

Words by LORENZ HART
Music by RICHARD RODGERS

217

TILL THE END OF TIME
(Based on Chopin's Polonaise)

Words and Music by BUDDY KAYE
and TED MOSSMAN

Slowly, with expression

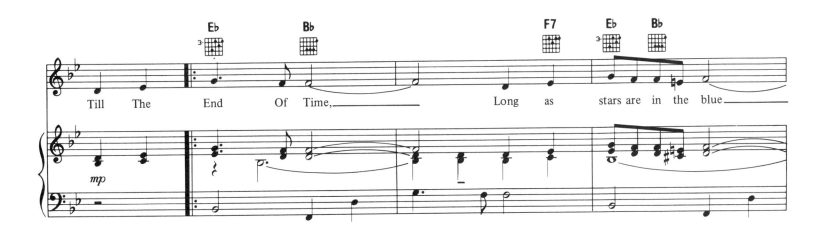

Till The End Of Time, _____ Long as stars are in the blue _____

Long as there's a spring, a bird to sing I'll go on lov - ing

YES! WE HAVE NO BANANAS

By FRANK SILVER and IRVING COHN

223

THE VARSITY DRAG

Words and Music by B. G. DESYLVA,
LEW BROWN and RAY HENDERSON

225

THERE'S A SMALL HOTEL

Words by LORENZ HART
Music by RICHARD RODGERS

YOU BETTER GO NOW

Words by BICKLEY REICHNER
Music by ROBERT GRAHAM

UP, UP AND AWAY

Words and Music by JIM WEBB

Moderately

Would you like to ride in my beau-ti-ful bal-loon?
world's a nic-er place in my beau-ti-ful bal-loon.
Love is wait-ing there in my beau-ti-ful bal-loon, It

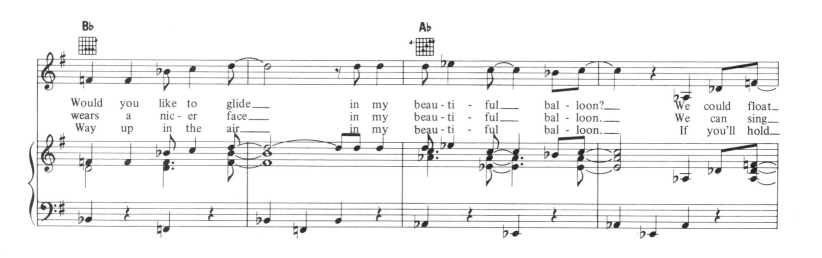

Would you like to glide in my beau-ti-ful bal-loon? We could float
wears a nic-er face in my beau-ti-ful bal-loon. We can sing
Way up in the air in my beau-ti-ful bal-loon. If you'll hold

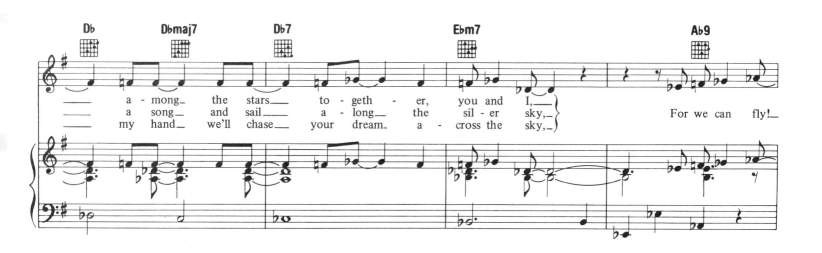

a-mong the stars to-geth-er, you and I,
a song and sail a-long the sil-er sky,
my hand we'll chase your dream a-cross the sky, For we can fly!

232

THE WORLD IS WAITING FOR THE SUNRISE

Words by EUGENE LOCKHART
Music by ERNEST SEITZ

234

235

YOU ARE BEAUTIFUL
(From "Flower Drum Song")

Words by OSCAR HAMMERSTEIN II
Music by RICHARD RODGERS

237

THEY CAN'T TAKE THAT AWAY FROM ME

Words by IRA GERSHWIN
Music by GEORGE GERSHWIN

THOSE WERE THE DAYS

Words & Music by GENE RASKIN

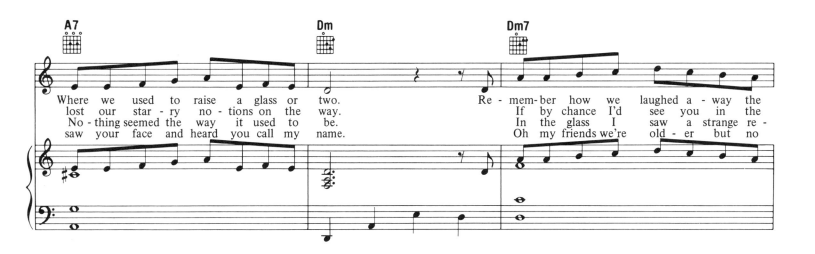

THE SOUND OF MUSIC
(From "The Sound Of Music")

Words by OSCAR HAMMERSTEIN II
Music by RICHARD RODGERS

STARTING HERE, STARTING NOW

Words and Music by RICHARD MALTBY JR.
and DAVID SHIRE

Quite slowly, with a steady beat

SPAGHETTI RAG

Words by DICK ROGERS
Music by GEORGE LYONS
and BOB YOSCO

SUDDENLY THERE'S A VALLEY

Words and Music by CHUCK MEYER
and BIFF JONES

WRAP YOUR TROUBLES IN DREAMS
(And Dream Your Troubles Away)

Words by TED KOEHLER and BILLY MOLL
Music by HARRY BARRIS

YOU NEEDED ME

Words and Music by
RANDY GOODRUM

Moderately